BINARY OPTIONS
BOOK OF KNOWLEDGE

Everything I Wish I Knew
Before I Started Trading

By Christopher D. Carlson

Copyright

Copyright © 2016 by Christopher D. Carlson All rights reserved. No part of this publication may be reproduced, distributed, or transmitted in any form or by any means, including photocopying, recording, or other electronic or mechanical methods, without the prior written permission of the publisher, except in the case of brief quotations embodied in critical reviews and certain other non-commercial uses permitted by copyright law. For permission requests, email the publisher, with the subject "Attention: Permissions Coordinator," at the following address. **mail@trainingforbeginners.com**

Disclaimer

Although the author and publisher have made every effort to ensure that the information in this book was correct at press time, the author and publisher do not assume and hereby disclaim any liability to any party for any loss, damage, or disruption caused by errors or omissions, whether such errors or omissions result from negligence, accident, or any other cause.

Earnings Disclaimer

Every effort has been made to accurately represent currency trading and its potential. There is no guarantee that you will earn any money using the techniques and ideas or software recommended in this publication. Examples in this document are not to be interpreted as a promise or guarantee of earnings.

Earning potential is entirely dependent on the person using the information, ideas, and the techniques. We do not purport this as a get rich scheme. Your level of success in attaining the results claimed in this document depend on the time you devote to the ideas and techniques mentioned, your finances, knowledge and various skills. Since these factors differ according to individuals, we cannot guarantee your success or income level. Nor are we responsible for any of your actions. Materials in this document may contain information that includes forward-looking statements that give our expectations or forecasts of future events. You can identify these statements by the fact that they do not relate strictly to historical or current facts. They use words such as anticipate, estimate, expect, project, intend, plan, believe, and other words and terms of similar meaning in connection with a description of potential earnings or financial performance. Any and all forward looking statements here or on any of our sales material are intended to express our opinion of earnings potential. Many factors will be important in determining your actual results and no guarantees are made that you will achieve results similar to ours or anybody else's, in fact, no guarantees are made that you will achieve any results from our ideas and techniques in our material.

Table of Contents

Introduction..1

What Are Binary Options?..3

How Is Binary Options Different Than Forex Trading?.............5

Tools For The Binary Trader..11

The Best Way To Look At Your Charts....................................35

Understanding Brokers...51

Strategies For Success..55

Trading Times And Lengths...71

How To Avoid Being Scammed..75

Signal Services..77

Conclusion...79

Terminology..81

Resources..83

Introduction

I have been trading Binary Options since 2012, and have been training, and helping people spot high probability setups since 2014. Having been educated in both traditional Forex and Binary Options trading, I have adopted a hybrid way of interpreting charts. During this time, I have had the opportunity to speak with many new traders, answering their questions, and helping them understand confusing aspects of Binary Options. Having a passion for teaching, I started to make a list of common questions and concerns, with the hopes of creating a book, or video series. This is why I created this no-nonsense, practical guide for beginners.

In this book, I use many terms that you may not be familiar with. I have included a list of definitions and links discussed, at the back of the book for your convenience. Depending on the method you use to view this book, the pictures may be difficult to see. To view them in better quality, visit

http://trainingforbeginners.com/binaryoptions/

There is also a disclaimer at the front of this book, not only for legal ramifications, but to help in your understanding that trading Binary Options is risky. I offer no guarantees that the information provided will lead to financial gain. This document is to be used as a training guide, and is in no way indicative of a trading system.

What Are Binary Options?

All-or-nothing options, fixed return options, and digital options are just some of the names commonly used to describe Binary Options. If you understand, there are people that make money when a currency changes in value, you are half way to understanding the concept of Binary Options. Forex traders buy or sell currency pairs, and hold their trade for days, weeks, months, or longer. I would describe Binary Options as the "hyperactive child of Forex." Binary trades are typically from one minute, on the very short end, to the end-of-day, being on the long end. The other main difference, you are not buying or selling anything. With a HIGH/LOW trade, you are simply predicting whether an asset will go up or down in value, over a set period of time. If you predicted correctly, you will be paid a predetermined percentage.

Is trading Binary Options for me?

I don't know your mindset or financial circumstances, but what I can tell you is, it's not right for everyone! When I first started out, I lost many trades, following useless strategies I found on Youtube. I used to feel physically ill every time a trade turned against me. I learned many hard lessons, and eventually lost all the money in my account. Having spoken with many new traders in the group I am involved with, I hear this story all too often. The one thing I was smart enough to do was, I only made investments with money I could afford to lose.

If you have an addictive personality, are considering using money you cannot afford to lose, or become stressed easily, I cannot recommend Binary Options to you. If after reading this book, you still want to try your hand at trading, you will need to adopt a professional mindset, study as much as you can about the markets and what moves them, you could become a trader. If you are unsure, try paper trading, this can be done without funding a live trading account.

Can I trade in my country?

In most countries you will be able to trade Binary Options. The problem is with the Brokers. The countries in which the broker operates can vary from company to company. Some do not operate within North America, while others do. While doing your research to find a reputable broker, it is important to verify they accept customers from your area.

How Is Binary Options Different Than Forex Trading?

Less capital to start with.

One of the many reasons Binary Options have become such a "hot commodity," is the fact that you can get started for $300 or less. This low barrier to entry has brought currency trading to the masses. For example; let's say we have deposited $300 in our new account, for $5 we can now open trades. (This will not be true for all brokers.)

Forex, on the other hand, requires a much larger initial investment to make any "real" money. It is however, possible to open an account for similar money to Binary Options. You could trade micro lots, but most experts would say, if you don't have a minimum of $1000 to invest, you will not get much benefit. In Forex, you make money from the amount the currency pair moves, so if you were to buy $5 worth of currency, and it moved, one one-hundredth of a percent in the direction you predicted you would not make much money. This is why Forex companies require you to trade in lots. This is a predetermined amount of money. I am over simplifying this, but the result is, you need more capital to make any real money.

You only need a sense of direction.

Binary options are much less intimidating for new traders. Most people trade Binary Options, using the High/Low feature. With this, you simply need to choose the amount of money you want to risk, direction the currency pair will end, and the time length of the trade. There are other ways to trade Binary Options, such as One Touch, and Range. These are for advanced traders, and will not be discussed here.

Forex takes a bit more knowledge to execute a trade. You need to know more than just the direction a given pair will go. You also need to have a good idea of how far it will go in that direction, and an understanding of lot sizes, among other things. If you are correct, with your direction prediction, but it does not move far, you will not make much, (if any) money.

Software learning curves.

With Forex, you usually have a way to execute trades via their website, but many FX (foreign exchange) traders choose to use the Metatrader 4 (MT4) platform, even though the learning curve can be steep. This is charting software that you install on your computer, which offers some benefits over the web-based solutions. With MT4, almost everything can be customized; from the colors, size of trend lines, chart templates, and profiles which can be easily saved with a few clicks of the mouse. To be a Forex trader you are required to learn many tools. Most online charts may allow you to add common indicators, such as; Bollinger Bands, MACD, or (RSI) Relative Strength Index. If you have visited Forex websites, you may have seen that many offer custom indicators for download. Unfortunately, these cannot be manually added. This is another benefit of the MT4 platform.

With Binary Options, it is all web-based, but most broker's charts are not very good. They are very small, and hard to read. It is impossible to add any indicators or even support and resistance lines. Metatrader 4 is used by most Binary Option traders that I know. Luckily, all of the more complicated features are not required to use this amazing charting software.

It's all or nothing.

Typically, if you lose your trade, you will lose the entire trade amount. This will depend on your broker, as some have started offering a small percentage (ex: 2%) on trades that are out of the money.

Trading with Forex, it is a very different system, so it is a bit hard to compare. You can specify the amount of money you wish to risk, by setting a "stop loss." You only lose that money if the price hits that value, if not you could possibly hold the trade until you are making profits. This scenario does not consider things like margin calls. There are a number of things to consider with Forex trading, which makes it more complicated than Binary Option trading.

Trade lengths.

With most Binary Option brokers, you can get one-minute, two-minute, five-minute, ten-minute, fifteen-minute, thirty-minute, one-hour, four-hour, and end-of-day trades. Some even offer thirty-second trades. You will need to do some homework, ensuring the broker of your choice offers the expiry times that will best satisfy your style of trading, and preferred strategies.

Trade lengths are one area where Forex shines. You can hold a trade as long as you want. For example, if you buy EUR/USD, and it starts to go down, no problem. As long as the price does not hit your stop loss, you can hold the trade until it goes back up to where you will make a profit. A typical Forex trade could last, from a few hours, to days, or possibly a few weeks, or even several months. This all depends on the type of trader you want to be.

Tradeable assets.

You can trade Currency (EUR/USD, USD/CAD, etc.), Commodities (Gold, Silver, Copper, etc.), Future Indices (Dow 30, S&P 500, etc.), and even stocks with most Binary Options brokers. Later in this book I will teach you about currency markets, and the best times to trade. This is important to know, as not all currency pairs or commodities are available to trade around the clock. This is dependent on if that market is open, the volume of trades being taken, and your individual broker.

The choices are slightly more limited in some ways with Forex. You do have a much larger selection of currency pairs to trade. You also can trade Commodities, and some Indices, but you cannot trade individual stocks. You can usually trade any currency pair your FX broker offers as long as the markets are open.

No trading fees.

There are no fees when dealing with Binary Options, but that does not mean they are a non-profit business. Most make their money from the trades that lose, some, such as CTOption, sell the trades in bulk to a bank, and they accept the risk of win/loss majority.

Forex fees are a bit harder to explain. If you understand that you make money when a pair moves in your direction, the FX brokers have what is called a "spread." This consists of two prices for a given pair. One is called "the bid price," this is the price people are ready to sell the asset for. The other is called "the ask price," this is the minimum price the sellers are willing to receive. To simplify, when you open a trade, you will be a few "Pips" (short for – Price Interest Points) in the losing direction, this is how they get their profit.

Note from the author.

I have listed the main differences between Binary Options, and traditional Forex trading. After reading these differences, you may have a misconception that I am anti-Forex. In reality, I think Forex has many benefits that Binary does not offer. As with everything in life, there are pros and cons. I have a Forex account, and love trading it, but it is not for a newbie.

Tools For The Binary Trader

Tools of the trade.

As mentioned earlier, the only tools you need are a web browser, and charting software. If you don't wish to install any software, you can use charts from "Free Stock Charts" **http://www.freestockcharts.com/** or from one of the other free services. I like the MT4 charts, so I will show you how to download, and install them for free.

Where can I get the MT4 charts?

There are many Forex brokers that offer free demo accounts. All of these demo accounts come with MT4 software. In the next example, I will demonstrate how to install charts from "FxPro" **http://www.fxpro.co.uk**

How to install MT4 charts.

After visiting the site in the previous section, you will be able to sign up for a DEMO account. Follow the steps shown in the accompanying pictures. (Occasionally the steps required may change on the website, but the process is fairly straightforward.)

1. Open website fxpro.co.uk

2. Click on "Online Trading."

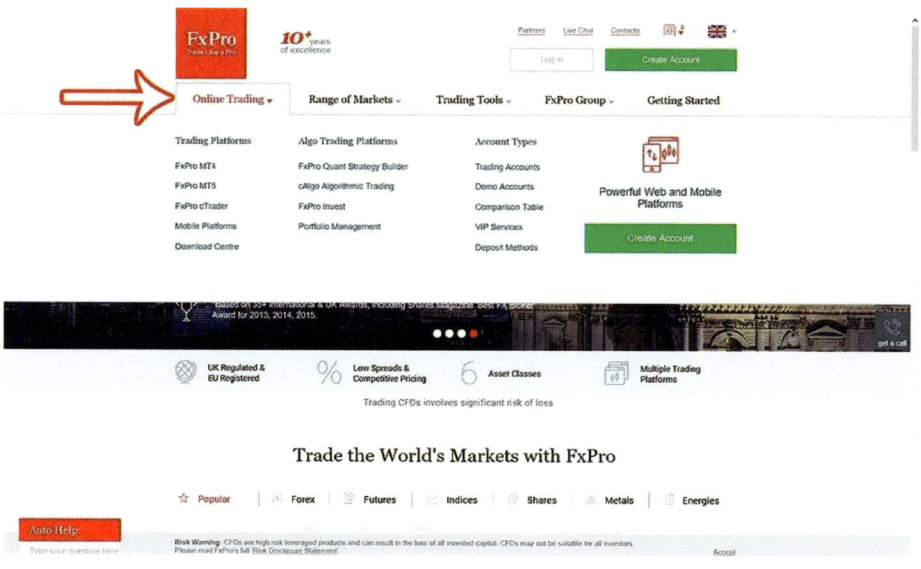

3. Click on "Demo Accounts."

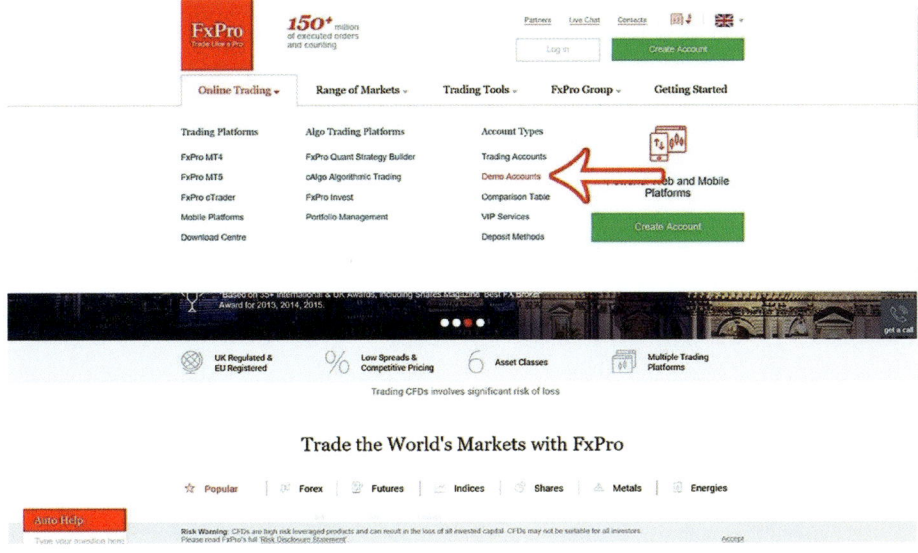

4. Fill out the form and click "complete."

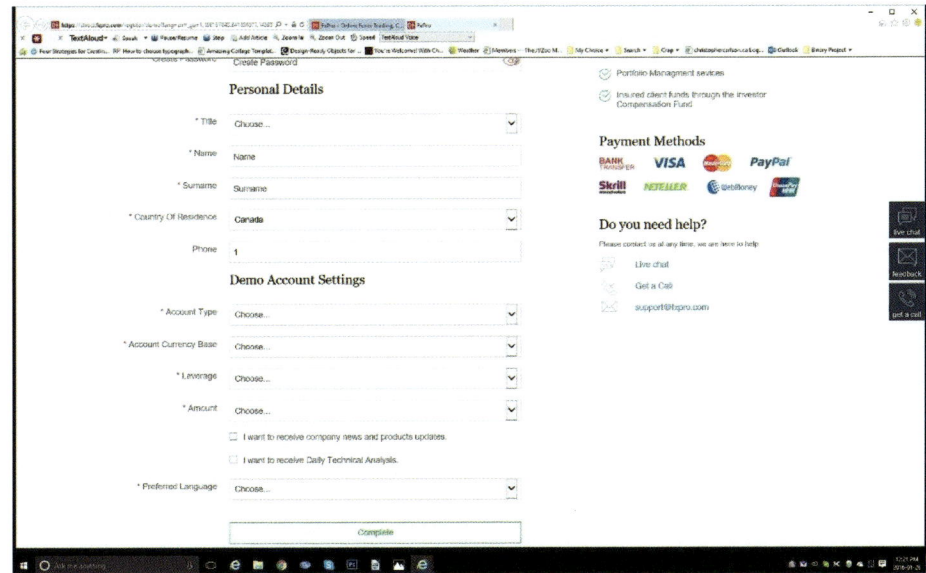

5. Click on the "Download FXPro MT4" button.

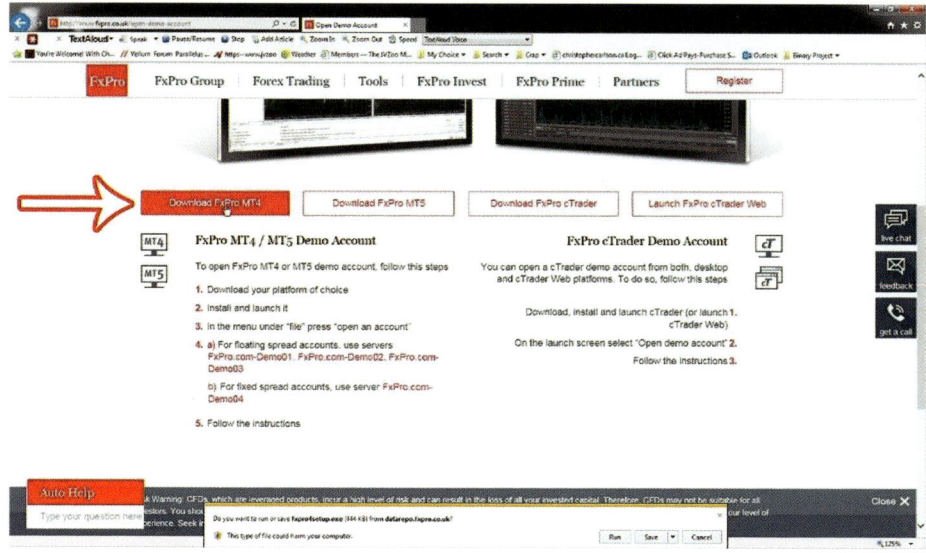

6. A "Welcome" box will open, click "next."

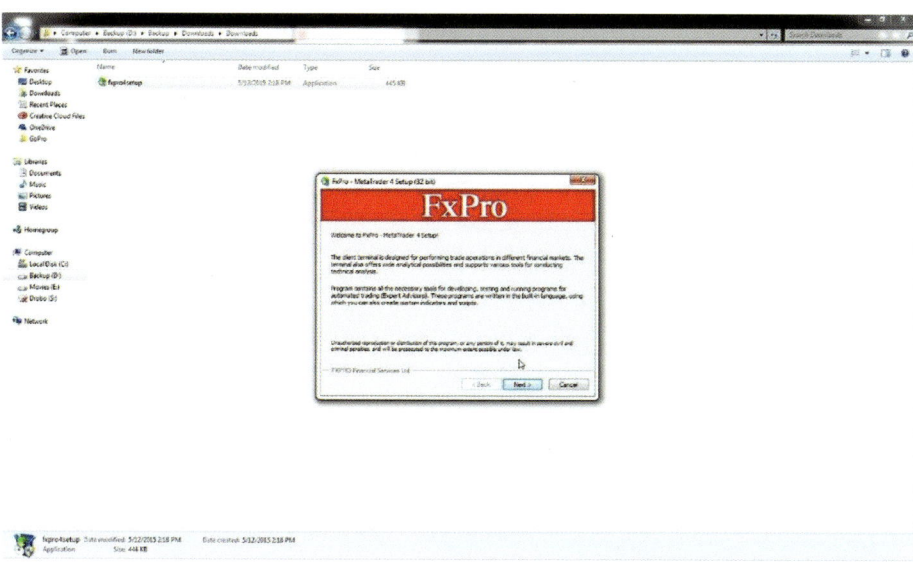

7. Click "Scan" and then when complete, click on the "demo server" with the smallest time.

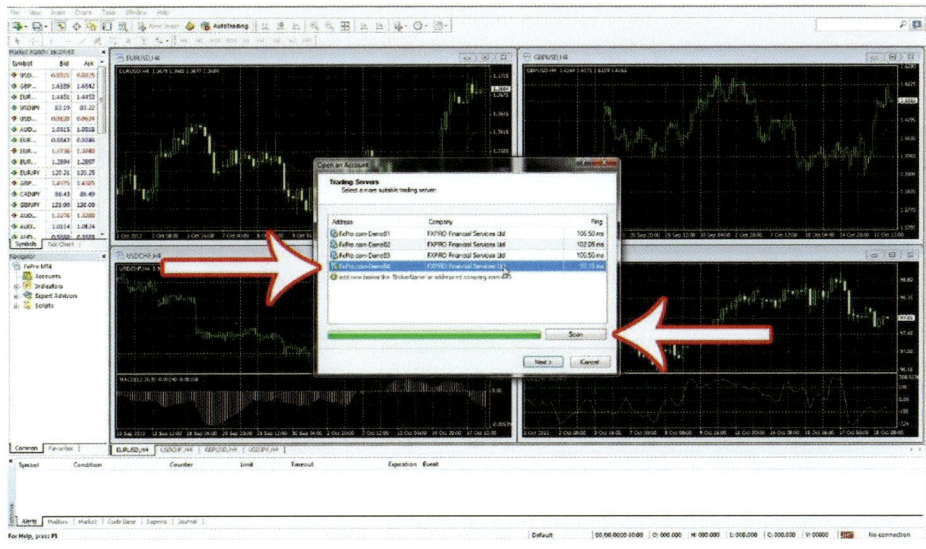

8. Select "New Demo Account" then click next.

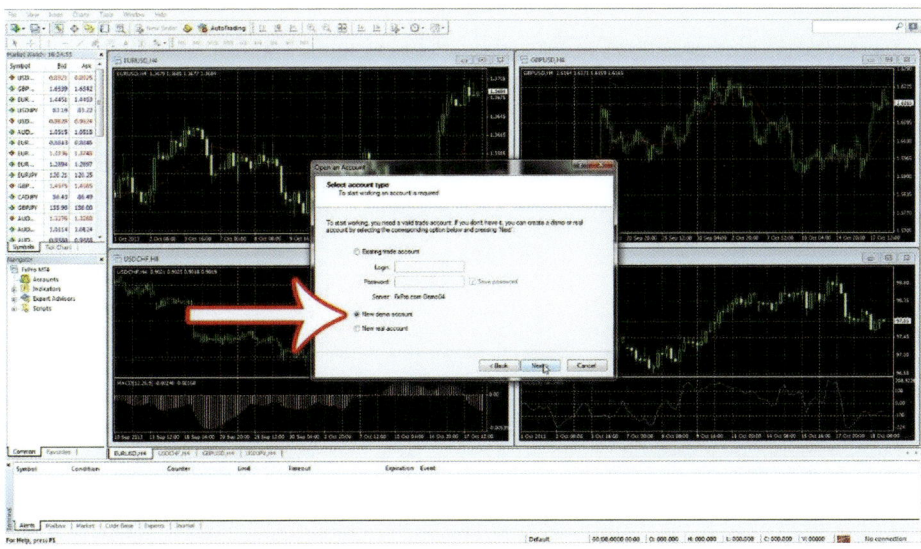

9. Fill out the information and click "I agree," click next. (If you would prefer not to use your real name or address, you can use false information.)

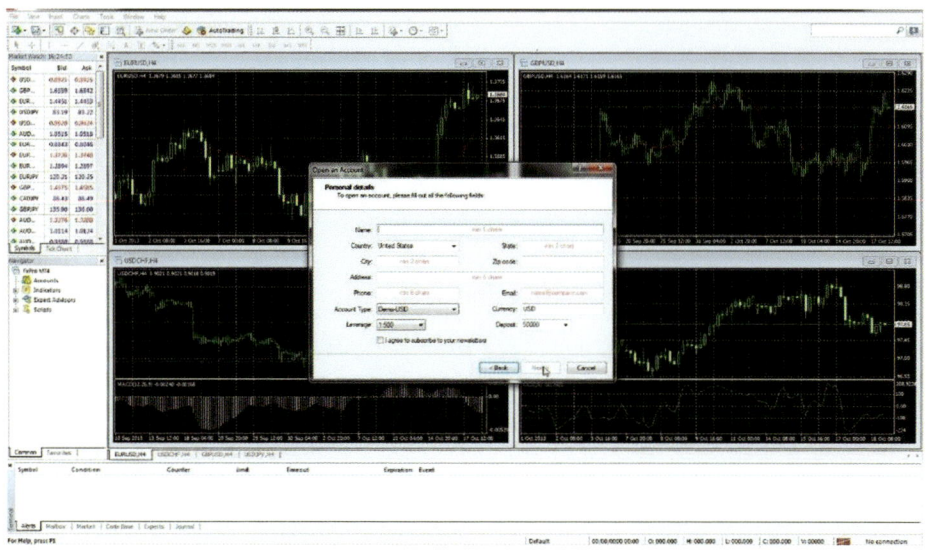

10. You are now given you "username and password," please write these down, as you cannot personalize them.

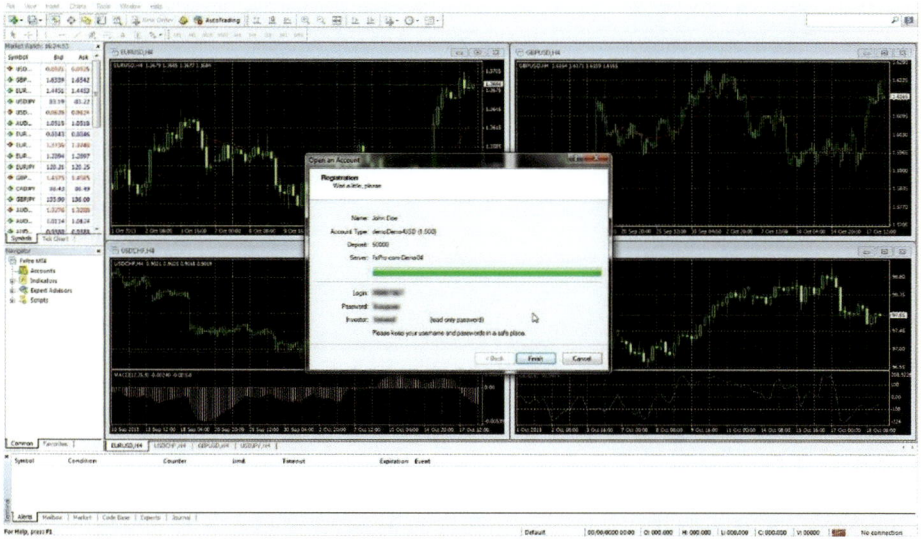

Adding charts to MT4.

1. If the "Market Watch" area is not open displaying the currency pairs available to be added, click the third button from the left to open it.

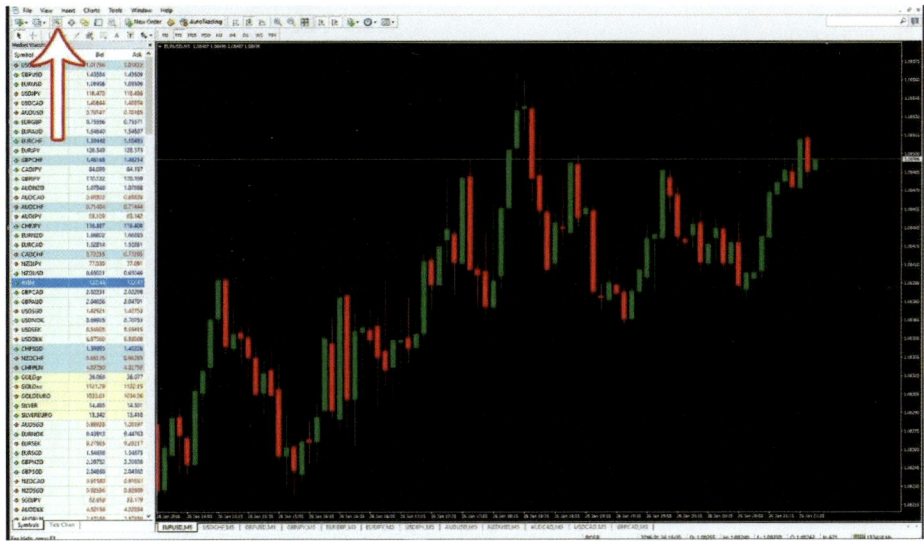

2. If you have newly installed MT4, you may see a very limited number of available pairs. To view all pairs, right click on any pair and click on "Show All."

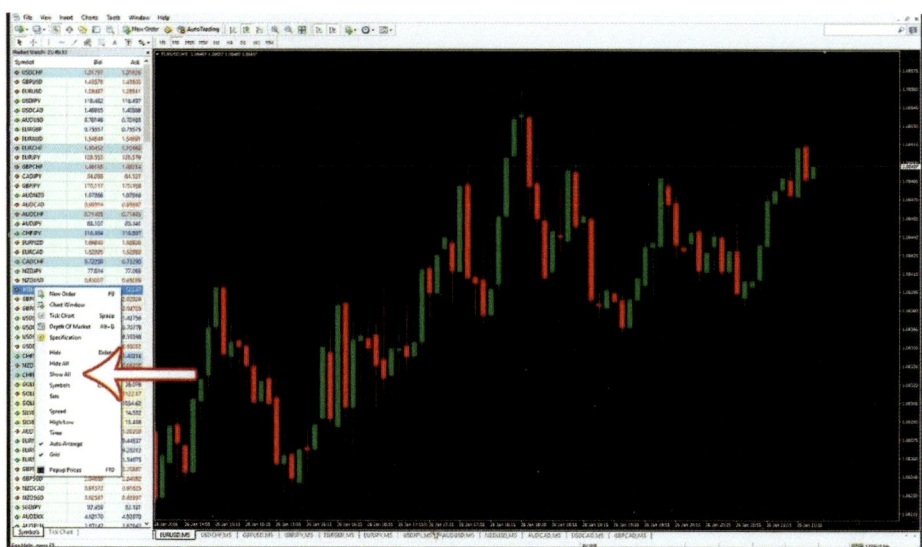

3. After you find the pair you wish to add, right click on it and chose "Chart Window."

4. Your desired pair will now be added for viewing. It will probably be displayed as a "Bar Chart" not "Candlesticks." The time displayed will usually be set to one-hour, therefore you will need to change it to your preferred time.

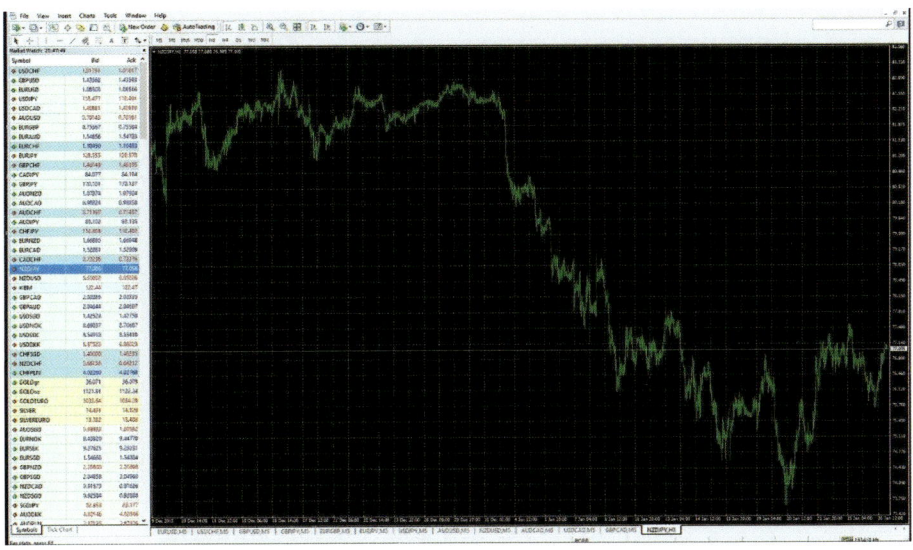

What pairs should I watch?

This will depend on the time of day you are trading, but the currency pairs I watch are: EUR/USD, USD/CHF, GBP/USD, EUR/GBP, GBP/JPY, EUR/JPY, USD/JPY, AUD/USD, NZD/USD, AUD/CAD, USD/CAD, GBP/CAD.

MT4 chart indicators, and templates.

When looking at most charts you will see an assortment of colored lines; some being straight, others curved, some horizontal, while a few will have vertical lines. Another set of symbols you may see are arrows, or even dots. Regardless of how they look these are all referred to as indicators, and are meant to give you indications on when an asset is about to change directions. MT4 comes with many free indicators that you can add to your charts.

Every trader is unique, and so is the way they prefer to have their charts laid out. If you, for example, look at eighteen different currency pairs, it can be very time consuming setting each one up. You may have to change the candle colors, add your favorite indicators, or even change settings in the preferences. This is where we can use templates. Simply set up a chart the way you like it, and save it to easily duplicate the setup on all your charts.

How to install indicators, and templates.

Pre-installed indicators.

Adding a pre-installed indicator is fairly straight forward. At the top of MT4, click on insert, indicators, and then choose the indicator you wish to install from one of the options provided.

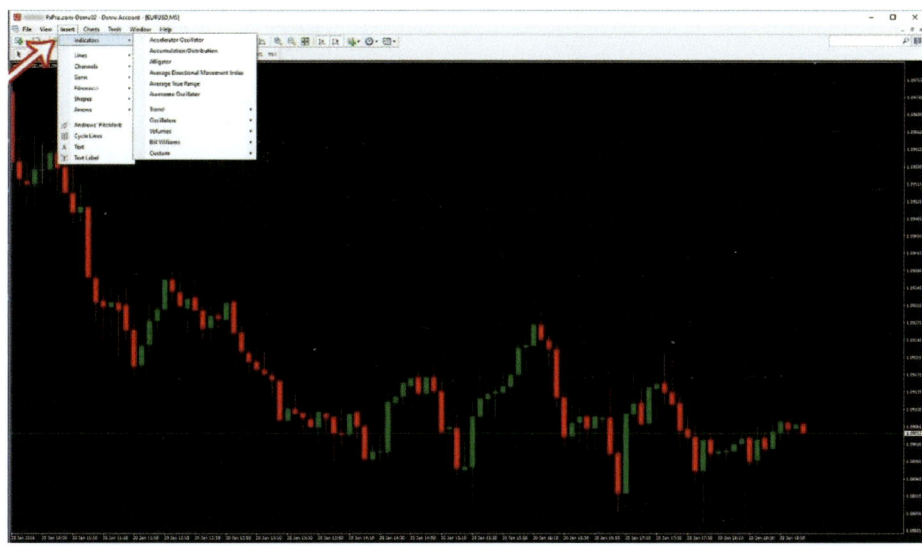

Non pre-installed indicators.

Not all of the indicators or templates you may want to use come pre-installed. The following pictures show how to get the files into MT4.

1. Open the MT4 software, and click on "File," then click on "Open Data Folder."

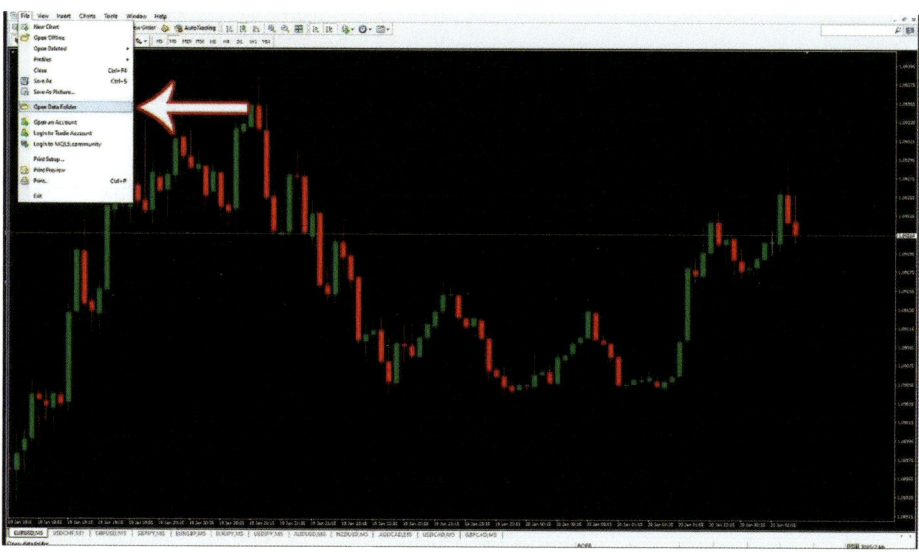

2. If the indicators you are trying to install include a template file, copy and paste it into the "templates" folder. If not, skip to the next step.

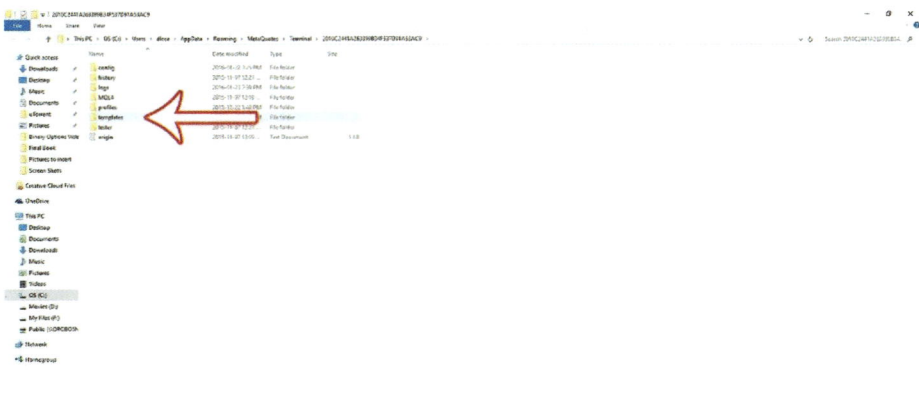

3. Double click on "MQL4."

4. Copy and paste the indicator files you want to install into the "Indicators" folder.

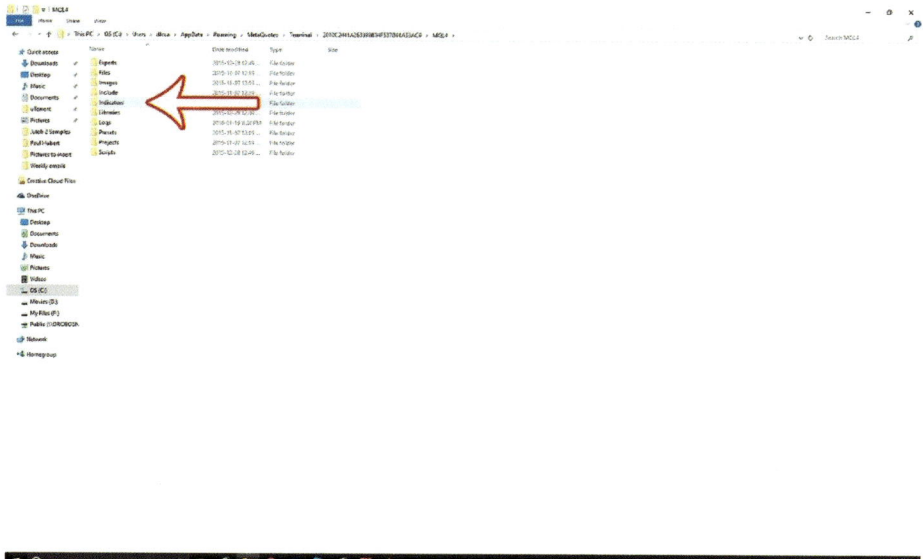

Your installed template and indicators should now be accessible, if not, close the MT4 software and reopen it.

A walkthrough of the MT4 platform.

MetaTrader 4 has plenty of features/buttons that aid Forex investors. Many of these are not applicable to Binary trading. In this section I will go over the most commonly used short cuts. We will start out by looking at the buttons found in the top area of the MT4 software.

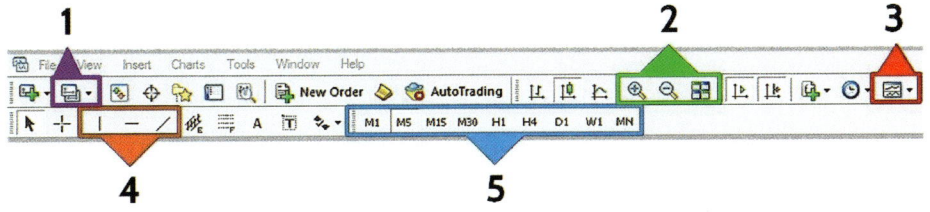

Button (1) is the profile button, this is an easy way to change chart settings on several charts at once.

25

Button (2) the zoom buttons.

Button (3) this is the template button, here you can see all of the templates you have saved. You also have the options to save, load and delete.

Button (4) line drawing tools for vertical, horizontal, and diagonal.

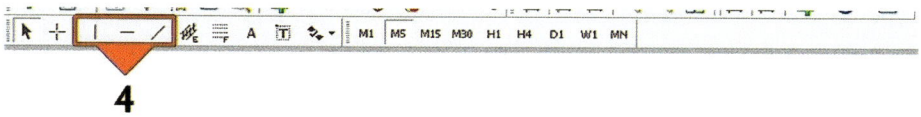

Button (5) this series of buttons changes how long each candle represents. Your choices range from one-minute to one-month.

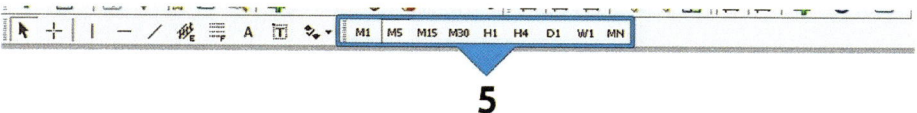

Profile button

(1) We start out with the profile button. This is one of the most useful buttons. Before I teach you how to set up a profile, I first need to explain what one is. As a binary trader, you may have many charts open at the same time. If you have them all set on the one-minute time period, for example, and want to switch them all to another time period, this can be labor intensive, as you would be required to switch each chart individually. With this handy feature, you can set up a different profile for each of the time periods you would like to observe, and switch between them with the click of one button.

Unfortunately, the setting up process is not as intuitive as you may think. For this example, we will set up two profiles, one that is one-minute, and one for five-minutes.

Setting up a one-minute profile.

1. Look at each chart, and ensure they are set to one-minute.

2. Click the profile button, then click "save profile as."

3. A dialogue box will pop-up, where you will enter a name for this profile. (We will call it Binary M1) Click "Ok."

Setting up a five-minute profile.

1. Click the profile button, then click "save profile as." (Naming this one Binary M5)

2. Look at each chart again, and switch them to the five-minute time period.

3. Verify everything is set correctly, by selecting the profile button, then click on "Binary M1" in the list. All your charts should now be set to one-minute. Click the profile button again, choosing "Binary M5" will switch to display five-minute charts.

A problem that will occur if you do not save your profile before setting the time periods is; the program thinks you are editing the profile that you currently have active. This is why I saved the five-minute profile before actually setting the charts to be five-minute. I did not want to edit the one-minute active profile.

Zoom buttons

(2) You will sometimes want to zoom in, and out on a chart. The first two buttons in this area accomplish that. The last button is used to tile your open chart windows.

Template button

(3) This is the template button. Once you have your chart the way you like, including your favorite indicators, and color preferences, you can save it as a "template." This button is where you save, and load a template to your chart. If you have multiple charts open, you will need to add the template to each separately.

Line tool buttons

(4) Here you will find three line tools. The first is vertical, it is used to mark a particular candle. The next two buttons are horizontal and diagonal. These are used to mark support/resistance areas.

Candle time buttons

(5) This group of buttons changes the amount of time each candle represents on the chart you have selected. The letter "M" represents minutes, and the "number" represents the amount of minutes before expiration of the candle. Minute time spans are one-minute (M1), five-minute (M5), fifteen-minute (M15), and thirty-minute (M30). Hourly candles are marked with the letter "H," and available as one-hour (H1), and four-hour (H4). Daily, weekly, and monthly are not as commonly used, but are indicated by (D1), (W1), and (MN). One thing that may not be evident is when exactly each candle is created. Some think the candle starts the second they click on the "Candle Time Button," but in actuality, you are viewing candles already progressing. (ex: If you click on the fifteen-minute button at 7:25 pm, that candle you see was created at 7:15 pm.)

Will the MT4 charts work forever?

Most Forex brokers require one demo trade, per thirty-day time period. If you do not know how to take a demo trade, follow these steps:

1. If the terminal window is not open at the bottom of your charts, click the 6th icon at the top of your page.

The window will open with many tab sections, select the tab labeled "trade" at bottom left of the page.

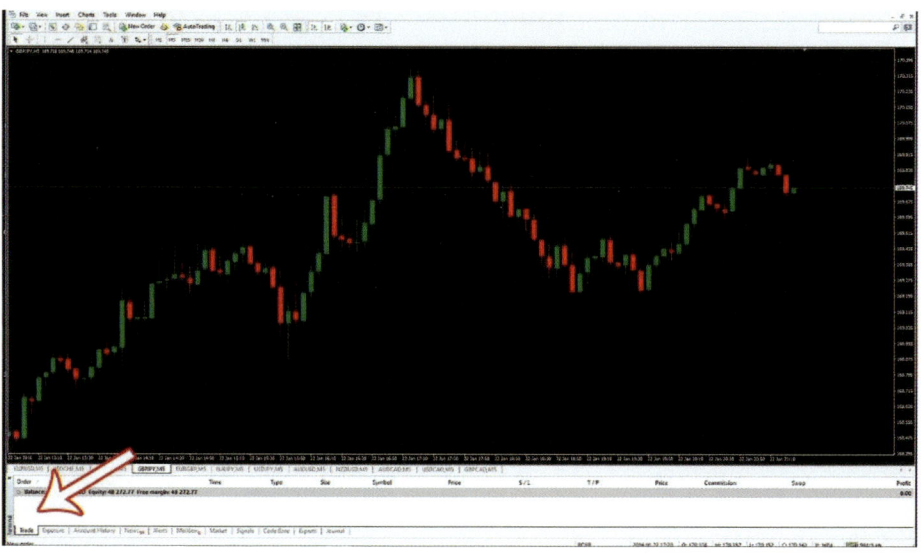

2. Right click in the center of your chart, and select "trading," then go to "new order."

3. A dialogue box will open giving you options to make a trade. Change the "volume" to 0.01, by using the drop down arrow.

4. Then click "Buy" or "Sell."

5. We will now close this order, by right clicking on the trade listed at the bottom in the terminal window. Select "close order."

6. If this is your first time closing a trade, you will get a pop-up with disclaimer notice. Click accept and then "OK."

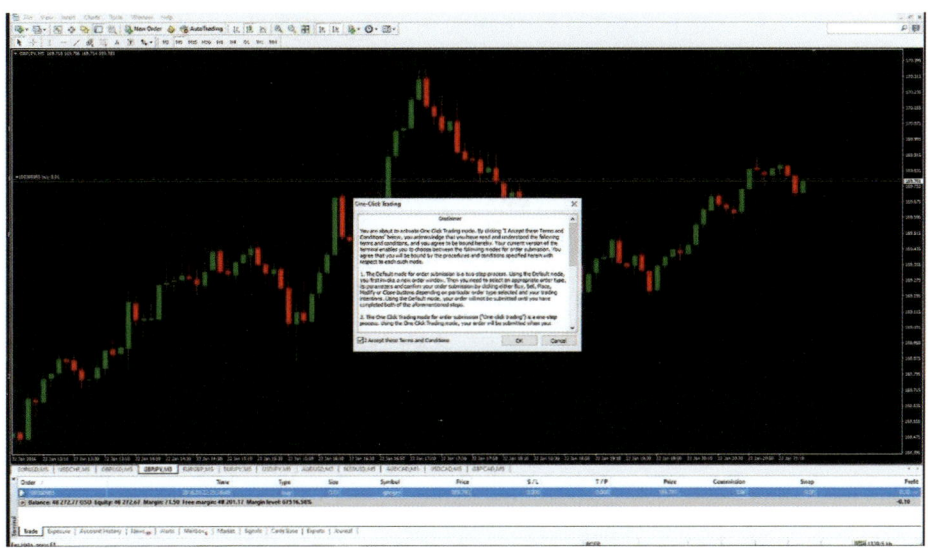

7. You will then be required to follow step 5 again.

If you have followed along with the instructions listed, you have just taken your first demo Forex trade. I am sure you will agree that it is complicated, especially for a new trader.

I have installed MT4, but the price differs from my Binary Options broker, why?

This is because MT4, and Binary Options brokers calculate differently. The price that is displayed on an MT4 chart is simply the "bid price." The way Binary Options broker's websites determine the price is different, because they need to incorporate the bid and ask price. The broker "Stockpair," determines the value by adding the bid and ask price, then divides by two. The sum is rounded to five digits after the decimal point. The way your broker comes up with its price, may differ.

Take screenshots.

It can be very beneficial to take screenshots of all the trades you take. Having a record of your charts to look back on, gives you the opportunity to learn from winning and losing trades, as your experience level grows. The software I use for this is, "Greenshots" found at: **http://getgreenshot.org/**

The Best Way To Look At Your Charts

When you look at the charts for the first time, there is a good chance they will be displayed as a bar chart. Bar charts, and candlesticks, both display the same information. Opening price, closing price, the highs, and lows reached during that time period. Although the same information is available, most people find candlesticks to be less confusing. (All future examples in this document will refer to candlesticks, but feel free to explore the other display types if you wish.) Below is an example of the differences between these two.

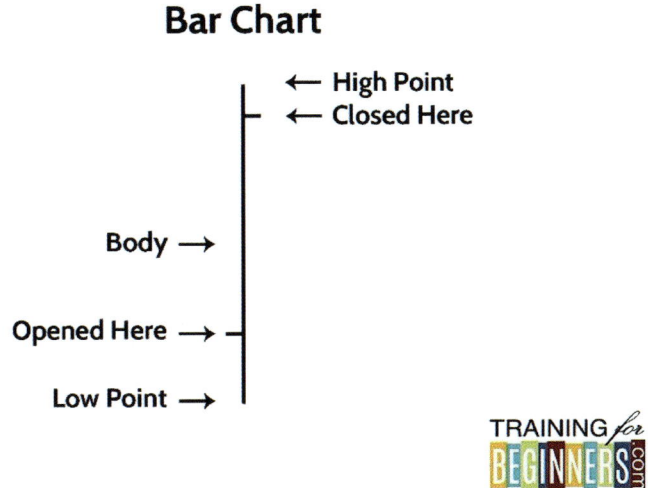

Candlestick vs. Bar Chart

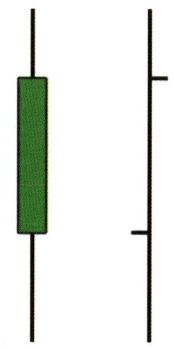

What is a candlestick?

A candle stick is a visual representation of the price movement during that time period. The body shows where the candle opened, and closed. The upper, and lower wicks show the highest, and lowest price for that candle.

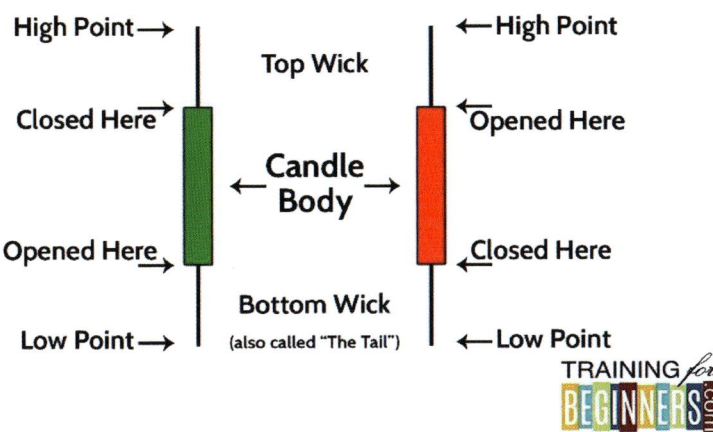

Understanding how, and why a wick is created.

A wick is created when the buyers/sellers, sometimes referred to as "Bulls/Bears," move the price of an asset in their favor, but encounter a stronger opposition. A candle may have different looks during its development, but we are only concerned with the completed candlestick. In the following diagram, I demonstrate how a large bottom wick is created. The candlestick labeled (1) represents where the candle opened, and moved down, temporarily creating a red bearish body. The price then shifted up above where the candle opened, as shown on the candlestick labeled (2). In the final picture labeled (3), the sellers made one last effort to push the price down, thus creating a small wick on top. With such a large wick on the bottom, this tells us the buyers were in control for this candlestick period.

Understanding the Wick

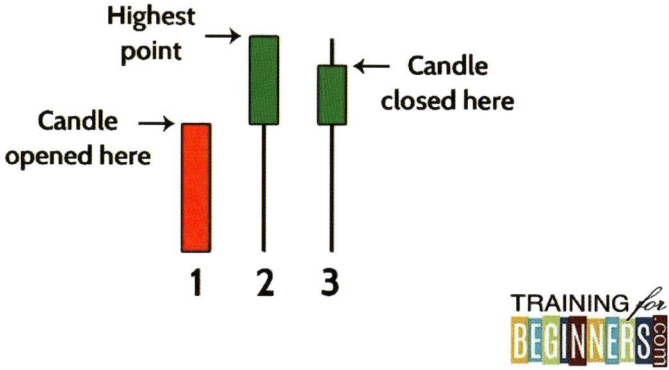

Large wick indicates one side is in control

Wick on bottom = buyers in control

Wick on top = sellers in control

Changing of the guard.

When looking at a chart, I always try to think of it as one army versus another. On one side, you have the Bulls / buyers, who want every candlestick to go up more than its predecessor. When the Bulls are winning the battle, you will see what is clearly an uptrend. There will probably be more green candles than red, at this point, with the majority being green.

On the opposite side are the Bears / sellers, their goal is to push the price down creating new lows. (When I first started out trading, I would sometimes get confused on the direction of the term Bulls and Bears. This story helped me remember: A Bull has horns and it throws the enemy up in the air. A Bear stands tall with arms out and bears down over its prey.) With this military mind set, I study the charts, evaluating who is in power, and looking for evidence of weakening. The most credible evidence will show up at places that have demonstrated good support, or resistance price action in the past. This is where I look for the four types of candlesticks that give the best indication that the guard (or direction) is potentially about to change.

Another thing I note is the size of each candle, in currency trading the size does matter! If I see larger green candles, (Bullish candles) but not by much, this indicates the Bulls are stronger, but could most likely lose power soon. If larger bullish candles are shown with meager red candles, I know I need to be patient, as the Bulls may be in control for some time. If I see a series of green candles, I look to see if their size is increasing or decreasing, as it will indicate whether the Bulls are gaining, or losing strength. In a ranging market, I examine the size of the candles after identifying the top and bottom of where the market is ranging. I then look to see if there is a bias to one side or the other. If it has been taking three or four candles to cross from the bottom of the ranging zone to the top, but has been taking five or six to reverse, this tells me the Bulls are stronger. I will then look for CALL opportunities.

Types of candlesticks to look for.

It has been said, "every picture tells a story," and this is true for candlesticks as well. Sometimes we can get a clear picture by examining a single candle, other times we need to look at a few candles to decode what the market is telling us. If we watch for the candle types listed below, in areas where we have drawn support and resistance lines, we can start to see high probability setups. (If you are unfamiliar with the concept of support and resistance, I will go over this in a future section.)

Engulfing:

An engulfing candle, is an opposing candle with a greater size body. This is, without a doubt, the most powerful single candlestick, therefore, my favorite in all of trading. Every other candle type requires more evidence of a reversal. This candle is usually the confirmation, "in and of its self."

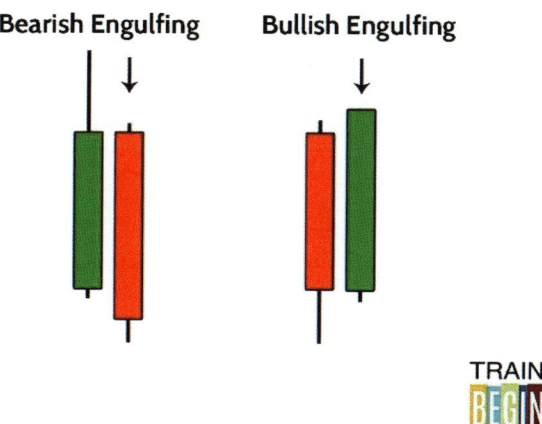

Pin Bar:

I would rate this as the second most important candlestick. A Pin Bar has other names, (ex: Shooting Star; Hammer) no matter the name you label it with, the Pin Bar is made up of 1/3 body, and 2/3 wick, either top or bottom. The color of the body does not matter. The large wick indicates a strong rejection of that price. If this candle is spotted near support/resistance zones, it is frequently preceded by a reversal in the trend.

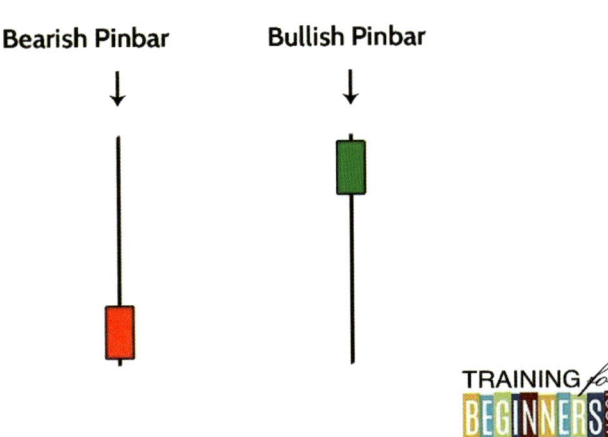

Doji:

The Doji is an indecision candle, a stale mate between the bulls, and the bears. It is a very small candlestick, without a body, resembling a "plus sign." By its self, it is not very useful, but combined with a support/resistance zone, and one of the other candlesticks (discussed in this section) you have yourself a very good indicator that the trend is potentially about to change direction.

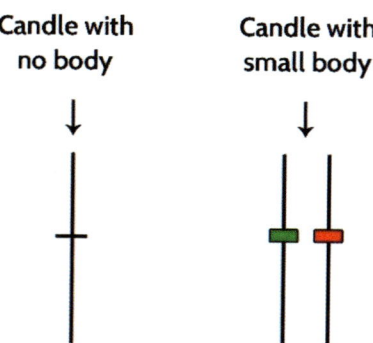

Railroad:

With this candlestick action, the bulls, and bears are in competition. If spotted at a point where we have placed our support, and resistance zones, it can give us a "heads up" of which way the trade will turn. A railroad candle is one that is almost the same size as the previous candle, only going in the opposite direction.

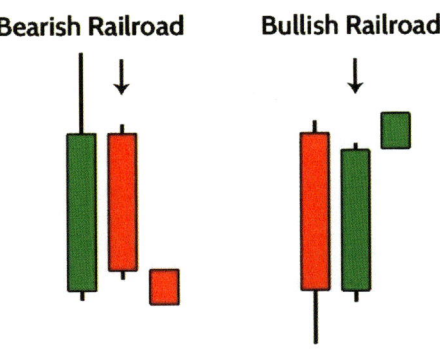

The Railroad Candle

Markets to look for.

After some time spent analyzing your charts, you will start to see that there are only three types of markets. They are:

Trending:

This type of market is easy to spot. In a down trend, the candles are consistently making new lows. Sometimes, the trend will be very strong, and all the candles together will look like a diagonal line. Other times, the movement down will look like "stair steps." Everything just mentioned is true in an uptrend, only opposite.

Ranging:

A ranging market is one that does not make new highs, or lows. The price does fluctuate, but stays contained within a range. It is possible to have wicks poke outside of the range area, but the body should close within that range.

The previous example demonstrated what a Ranging market would look like, when it is going sideways. This is not the only way you may see "Ranging" on your charts. The following example shows what a Downtrending Ranging market looks like.

Sideways (flat):

This market is similar to ranging, but without the price movement. Often times you will see a red candle followed by a green candle, in a repeating pattern. These candles are normally very small. This type of market is very difficult to trade. With so little movement, it would be impossible to predict where the price will be at the end of a trade.

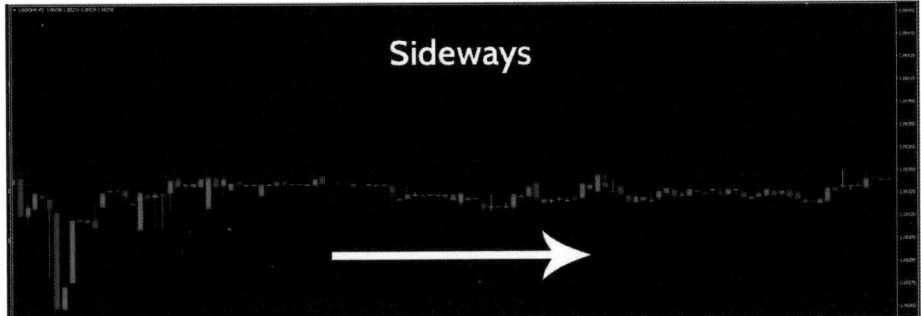

Accessing the charts.

New traders are sometimes amazed at the speed in which I can look at a chart, and decide if there are any trade opportunities. Now that you have a better understanding of the types of candles, and types of markets available, I would like to walk you through the process of how I quickly assess a chart.

The first thing I look at is the size of the candles, if I am seeing Doji's, and other small bodied candles, I stay out, and move on to another currency pair chart. If they are a decent size, I take the next step in my mental checklist of required components.

My second step is to look at the color of the candles; this is to determine if a trend is happening. If neither the Bulls nor Bears are in control, you will see the red/green candles alternating. This is a sign of indecision, and it is best to hold off taking a trade.

If all signs are good, I will look around to see the history of the sticks. Have they been heading in one direction for a very long time, without retracing? The pattern I like best is when you see the candles zig-zagging on the chart. This is the textbook behavior on how the candles should move. For example: If EUR/USD is in a down trend, we like to see it drop, retrace a little, then drop even more. This can continue for sometime, and can make a pair very predictable.

When looking over the history, I also check areas where it has turned around. At these reversal points, (also known as support and resistance) I observe if at least one of the four candlestick patterns is present. Finding these indicators adds confirmation that the chart is behaving as expected.

The last step I take before placing a trade, is to look for the nearest S/R zone, then watching to see if any of the tell-tale candlestick patterns emerge. If so, I take the trade.

If you are a more advanced trader, you can also incorporate MT4 indicators. RSI and Stochastic are two of the most popular.

If you are interested in adding indicators to your charts, it is important to realize two facts. The first being, indicators are only as good as your understanding on how to interpret the data they provide. Gaining as much information as you can on these tools will help you immensely. Secondly, all indicators are lagging, and use data from previous candles. This can help you make better decisions on what may happen next, but it is not a "crystal ball," therefore, it cannot predict the future.

When new traders start using these more advanced tools, many become blinded by how straightforward they appear. There is no guarantee the market will turn in the direction expected, it is still an educated guess as to what will happen.

Understanding Brokers

What is a broker?

A broker is the company where you make your trades.

Choosing a broker.

It all starts with choosing the broker. Many companies claim to be "the best" out there. Where your head will start to spin, is when you start reading reviews, and doing the research to find a truly reputable one. Many people write good reviews for bad brokers, and products, just for the affiliate commissions. You will most likely see positive, and negative comments for every broker you research. So how is one to know the best choice to make? My advice would be to ask other binary options traders who they are with, and if they have had any trouble withdrawing funds. I have used three different brokers in the past with mixed results. One made it impossible to withdraw, one had a very high, $25 minimum trade amount, and the one I settled on has given me no problems. You can invest as little as $5 per trade if you wish. (If you would like to learn more about my favorite broker, please visit:

http://trainingforbeginners.com/binaryoptions/

What is the minimum amount I can start with?

Before I answer this you really need to understand money management, but due to my broker, CTOption allowing $5 trades, I would say good money management would allow for a minimum amount of $300. Your finances are your responsibility and your personal decision. Remember, never invest and trade with money you cannot afford to lose.

What is money management?

Although this is not a fun topic, it is a necessary one if you want to have longevity in trading. As a new trader, you will probably want to start seeing big improvements in your account immediately. As natural as this type of thinking is, without curbing this impulse you will end up broke. In order to build an account fast, you would need to risk a very large percentage of your capital on each trade. If you could be guaranteed to win, this would be acceptable. Trading comes with no such guarantees. We must learn to trade smaller amounts, and have our accounts build slower. The common accepted rule is, only risk 2% – 5% of your balance on a single trade. This is one reason why it is better to start with a bigger balance.

Another reason why some people recommend this, is that it reduces your exposure to the market. The more you trade, the higher the risk of losing. (ex: If $24.00 is placed on a trade, and it wins, $17.28 is what you would have profited. Not everyone can afford to risk $24.00 at once. If you are only able to place trades for $12.00, you would need to take two trades to earn the same amount, but if you lost one of these trades, you would be "in the hole," for $3.36.) All examples are calculated using a payout of 72%.

The final piece of advice I have regarding this topic is to be consistent with the amount you trade. Mathematically, it is better to pick an amount and stick with it. For example; if you were to win seven out of ten trades, and risk $10 on each, you would profit $20.40. (With a payout of 72%.) If you were inconsistent with the amount wagered, bidding $5 on some trades, and $20 on others, you would soon see this is a losing strategy. If you were to lose on the $20 trades and win on the smaller $5 trades, you would be out of the money, even with a 70% win rate.

The example above is calculated with a 72% payout. One thing that complicates these examples is the time of day your trade takes place. The Asian Session (6 p.m. – 3 a.m. EST.) has a payout of approximately 65%, with some brokers. Always keep this in mind as it may dramatically change the amount of profit you see.

Understanding currency pairs.

When trading Binary Options, or Forex, it is beneficial to have an understanding of what you are actually trading. You are literally trading one currency with another. This is why you always see two currencies together (ex: USD/CAD). The first half (USD) of the pair is called the "base currency," and the last half (CAD) is called the "quote currency." The price shows the amount of money needed to purchase one unit of the "base currency." For example; if the price of USD/CAD is 1.41000 you are buying one American dollar, for $1.41 Canadian.

What is better for Binary traders, technical analysis or fundamental analysis?

As a Binary trader, who primarily trades currency pairs, you will be mostly using technical analysis. This is the art of studying the charts, looking at candlesticks, and candlestick patterns for good setups. The fundamental analysis that I do, is starting my trading day looking over the news events scheduled for that time period. I then check to see how much of an impact they are believed to make. It is at this point when I decide if I am going to trade the news, or stay out of all trades during this time period. Having a better understanding of how world events can have an impact on the currencies that you trade, will give you an advantage. For example: If you see news related to oil prices around the world, it can affect the Canadian dollar, as they are one of the largest exporters of oil.

Strategies For Success

Start out with a ritual.

When I start out my morning trade session, there are five things I always do before I take my first trade:

1. I open up a spread sheet, where I chart my wins and losses.

2. Open up my MT4 software that has the charts set to five minutes. (Have a quick look to see if any significant movements have happened since I last checked.)

3. Open another MT4 chart that is set to fifteen minutes, and look through it.

4. Check for news at "Investing.com", for events that are scheduled during the time I will trade.

5. Login to my broker.

It is at this time I start to look for potential trade setups. The way you start your trading session may not be the same as mine, but I would highly recommend using a spread sheet to chart your trades. Other information I would document would be; wins/losses, times of day, lengths of trades, currency pairs, direction of trades. After studying my trade log, I was surprised to learn, I lose more CALL trades, than PUT. I now rarely look for CALL setups.

Set goals.

It is always a good idea to set goals when it comes to trading. When first starting out, your goals may be to look at the charts for thirty-minutes per day, and take one demo trade. The more confident you feel about your abilities to predict the direction a currency pair will go, your goals should change. It is at this point when you should start to take trades with real money. For example; if your goal is to take three real trades per day, but the market is not showing you high probability setups, never forget your ultimate goal, to MAKE MONEY!

Know when to quit.

There are some days no matter how good the charts look, you just can't seem to win! It is tempting to keep trying, and make back your losses, but this is the plan of a "fool." I was always taught, if you lose twice, in the same session, call it quits for the day. This can also be good advice for times of successful trading. If you win a few consecutive trades, you may be wise to stop trading. Two winning trades are better than, two wins and one loss.

Demo accounts can cause bad habits.

If you choose to open a Binary Options account, check to see whether the broker will also give you a "demo account," and for what time period. I do recommend that everyone gets one, but they can come at a cost. Psychologically, there is a difference between trading with demo dollars, and actual money. Even I take trades on my demo account, that I would never consider with my real one. They are best used to develop new strategies, but they can teach you to be reckless. When trading with a demo, behave as if it is real.

The trend is your friend!

In a trending market it is common to have thoughts like: "This can't go much higher. I will open a PUT trade; This has been dropping for quite a while, it has to be ready to turnaround. I will open a CALL trade." Although there are indicators that can be added to your MT4 charts that can help indicate when a turnaround is about to happen, few are accurate in a trending market. It is easier to go "with the grain," than against it. Too many people make the mistake of trying to pick the very top or bottom of a trend. You will have a higher probability of success if you simply, "go with the flow."

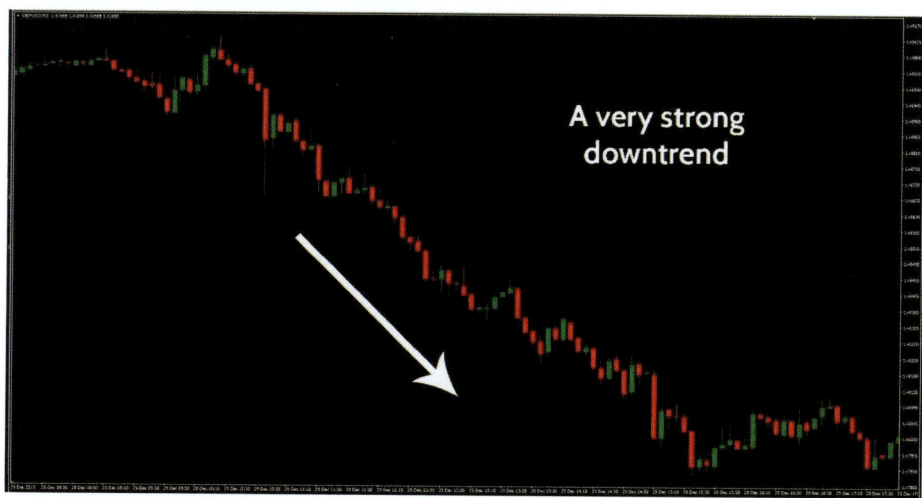

Support and resistance.

Forex traders have long recognized the importance of charting support and resistance (S/R) zones. These zones can give real insight as to which direction the market may swing. As humans, we tend to be creatures of habit. Currency traders have these same tendencies, and by looking for areas where traders frequently reverse the direction of any given asset, this can give us a considerably better idea of where to enter. Trades incorporating S/R can have a much higher probability of winning.

"Support" is a zone that is below a current assets price. Think of this line as if it were the floor of your house. Areas that have been drawn above the current price are called "resistance," and should be thought of as your ceiling.

The big traders, such as banks and institutions, are certainly looking at the weekly/daily S/R zones. These are definitely the most accurate chart time frames to draw from, but that does not mean we cannot obtain great information from lower time frames. The real question is, how low can we go while still finding accurate S/R areas? As a general rule, I would not use (by itself) anything less than a line drawn on a fifteen-minute chart. If a currency pair I am looking at, is about to hit a line I have drawn on the fifteen-minute chart, I will quickly look at the thirty-minute, and one-hour time periods. I check to see if they additionally show this as an area of possible reversal. If I am trading off of the five-minute chart, I will also note if this area shows signs of S/R. If one other chart is in agreement, I then look for my favorite candlesticks to appear, when they do, I will take the trade. If they do not agree, I make my decision based on the other merits of the setup, such as; candlestick patterns, candlestick sizes, and MT4 indicators.

One trick you may find useful when placing S/R lines, is to first look at the daily charts, and place your lines with one color. Then switch to the four-hour time charts, and use a different color, moving on to the other time periods, adding a unique color for each. This will give you the ability to know at a glance what time period that zone is on, the higher the time period, the more reliable it is.

In this example, I will give you a typical scenario; EUR/USD is in a downward trend. We have drawn a line of support that we believe it may bounce off of, if it does, great! If it continues its move down through our line of support, I would wait for it to come back up, and see if it can go through this line, which is now a resistance area. There are occasions where a currency pair will just over extend itself, and react as we thought it would, only a little late. I would expect it to bounce off of this line and continue down. Just to be clear, when a line of support is broken, and new candles are created below our line, that line now becomes "resistance." This is also true for assets that are in an upward trend, if a line of resistance is crossed convincingly, (more than a few pips) that line would become "support."

Predicting what happens after an asset breaks through support or resistance can be difficult. It has been my experience that you will frequently see the following: If a currency pair is on a down trend, and breaks a line of support, (as illustrated from 1 to 2) it will at some point retrace, (as illustrated from 2 to 3) and go back up to what is now a line of resistance. After it hits that line, in most cases, it will go down even further. (as illustrated from 3 to 4) The same is true for an uptrend, only in reverse. What was once support, can become resistance, and vice versa.

Breaking Support or Resistance

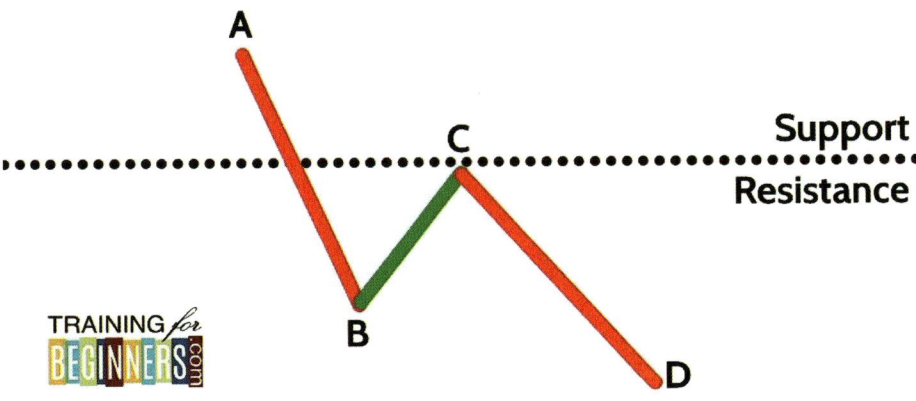

If you have noticed, I always referred to these areas as zones. This is because there is some confusion as to how an asset may respond to a line we have placed on the chart. Sometimes, you will see a currency pair touch, and bounce off a line as if it was a ball, hitting the pavement. Other times, the reversal will happen early, late, or not at all. As accurate as these zones can be, this does not mean every S/R area will be respected. It is important to note that some currency pairs highly respect these zones, while others are much looser. By logging each trade in a journal, you will come to understand the characteristics of each currency pair, and how they react to S/R zones.

If you would like to learn more about S/R, I would recommend subscribing to "Forex Reviews" on Youtube. Find his channel at: **http://trainingforbeginners.com/forexreviews**

Drawing support & resistance.

It is all well and good to promote using S/R zones, but if you do not know where to place the lines on your chart, it is of no help. One trick I learned was to switch your candlesticks into lines. This makes it much easier for the beginner to spot the areas we are looking for.

1. Right click in the center of your chart, and select "Properties."

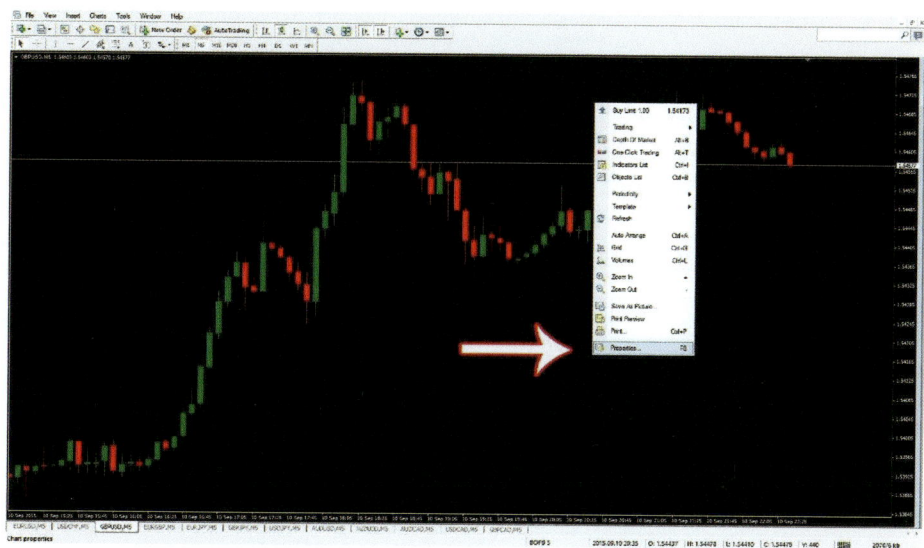

2. Click on the "Common" tab.

3. You will see "Candlestick" selected.

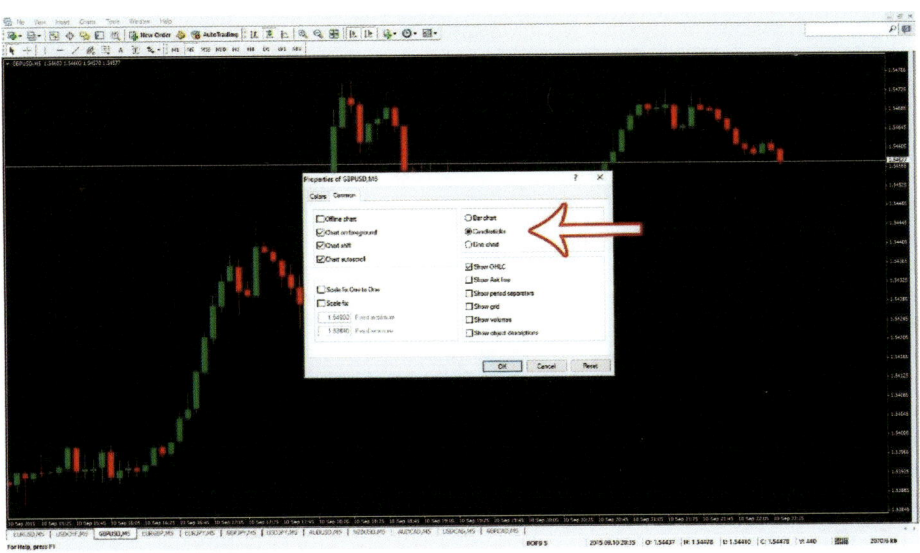

4. Select "Line chart," and then click "Ok."

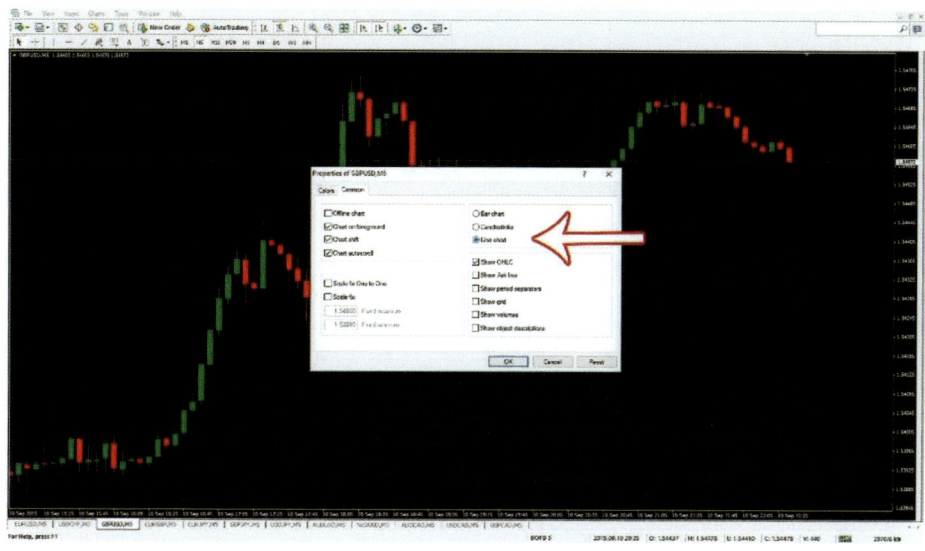

5. You will now see your candlesticks have been replaced with a solid line. It is at this point, you can start using the horizontal line tool. Look for areas that have touched a zone multiple times. Always keep in mind these are zones, not brick walls. In this example, you can see the price has moved past my line labeled (1.), but not by much. This is why I would still consider this valid. Areas marked (2., 3., and 4.) are all at about the same height. In (5.) on the other hand, you can see this price turns slightly before the line I have drawn.

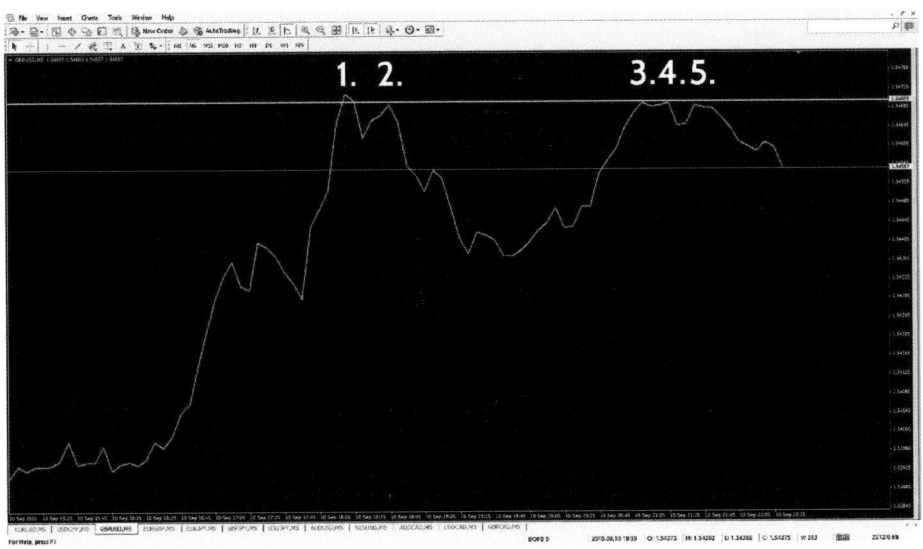

6. In this image, I have added my resistance line. Label (1.) is touching the line as resistance, and labels (2., and 3.) touch the line as areas of support.

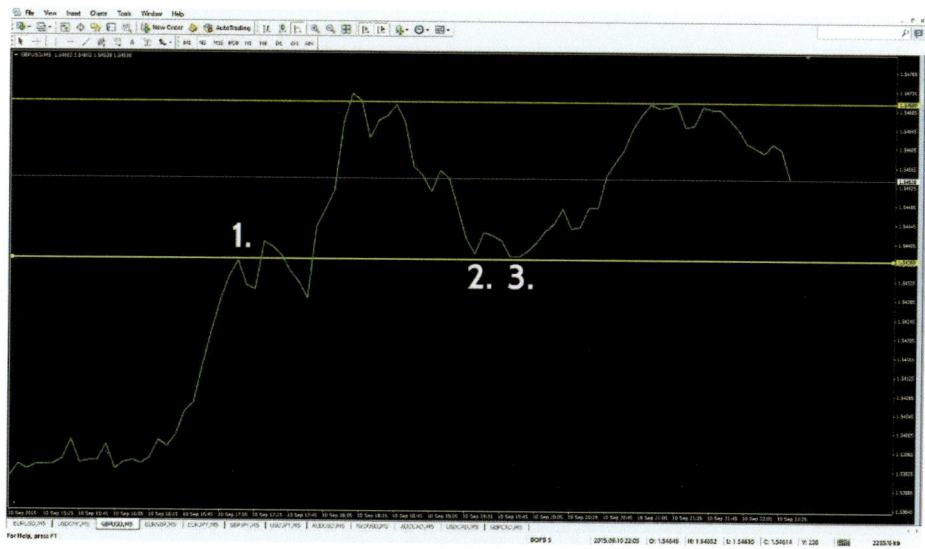

7. Now you can turn your candlesticks back on, by following the steps in reverse above. It is at this point that you may want to move your S/R lines slightly, to fit properly.

Changing the appearance of your lines.

In an earlier section I discussed a trick for viewing S/R lines for different time periods, by changing their colors. This is how to do that.

1. After adding a horizontal or vertical line to your chart, you may want to change it's color, thickness, or whether it is solid or dashed.

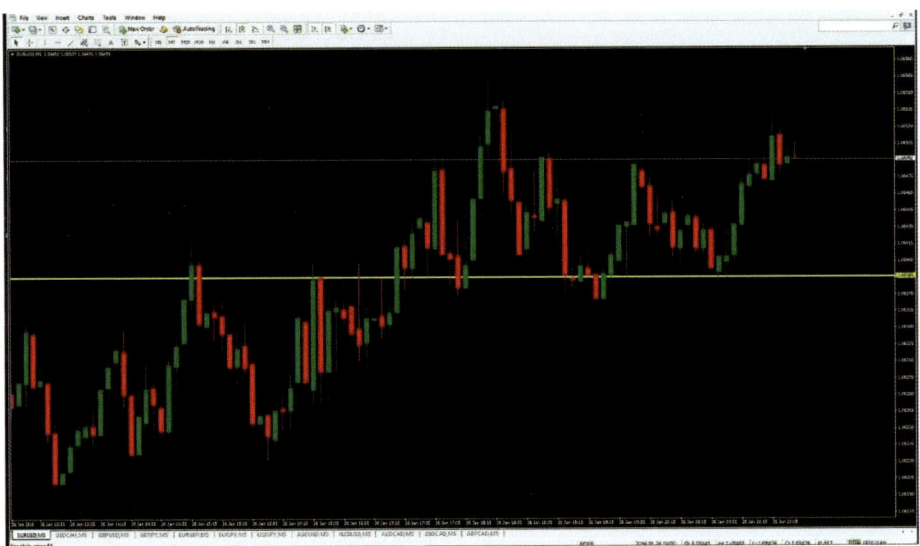

2. You first need to make your line active by double clicking on it. Once active you should see a "dot" at the beginning and end of the line.

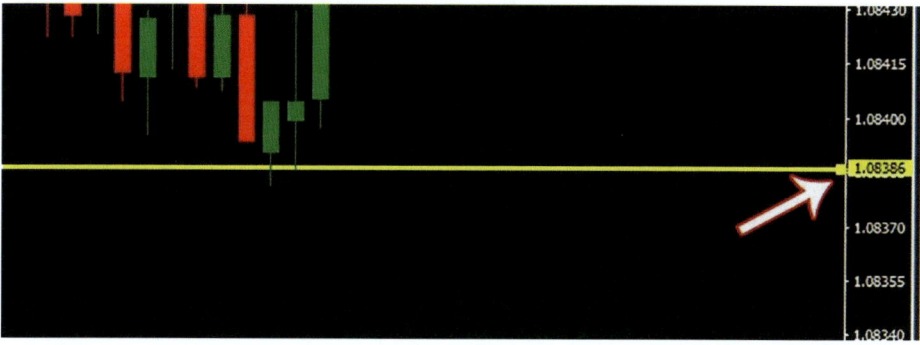

3. Left clicking on the line while it's active will allow you to move it on the chart, right clicking on the line while it's active will display a dialogue box. If you wanted to delete the line, you would choose that option. To get to the color settings, in our example, click on "Horizontal line properties."

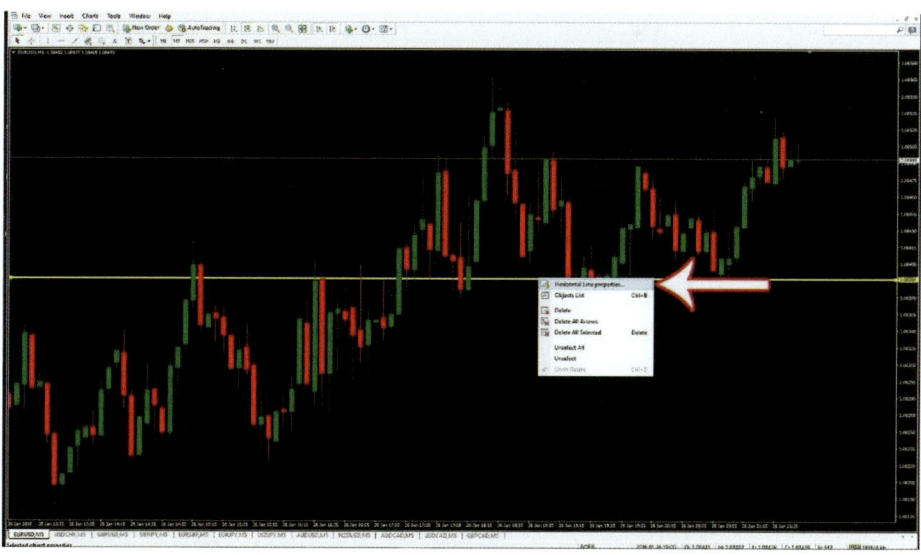

4. Under the "Common" tab you will find the options available to change your lines appearance.

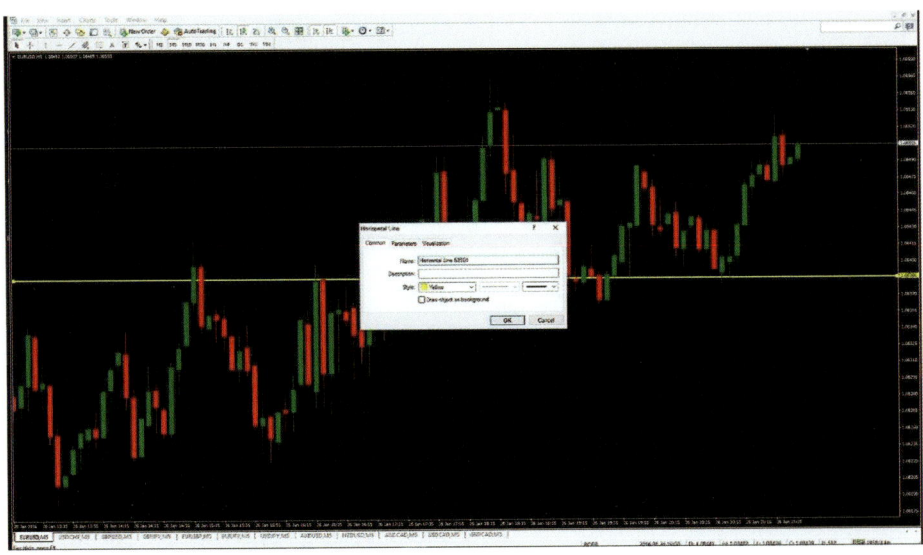

Keep your eye open for patterns.

Many times the charts may look chaotic to you, often times they are. One exercise you can try, is to see if there are any patterns that have formed previously. Are these patterns continuing? When price movement is being somewhat predictable, this is when patterns emerge, and can be a great time to trade.

In the following example, you can see a strong downtrend that has created a typical support/resistance pattern. Starting at label (1), there is a downtrend, that last five candles. Label (2) shows a single candle going up, that is large. This is commonly called retracement. The downward movement starts immediately, labeled (3), and moves down past our previous lowest point to label (4). An unusually large, single upward candle retraces back to the earlier lowest point, labeled (2). I have marked this area with a white horizontal line pointing out the S/R area. Finally, another move down is demonstrated from label (5) to label (6). This pattern of dropping, retracing, dropping farther may continue for hours, or may stop without notice. It is our job as traders to spot these trends, and act accordingly.

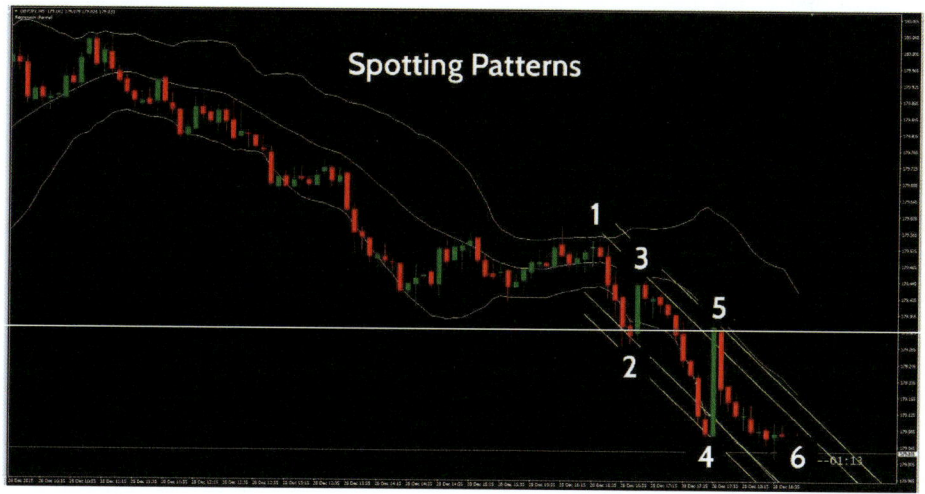

Trading Times And Lengths

Best and worst times to trade.

When starting to learn about currency trading, it is natural to want to learn the best strategies for success. Knowing how, and why a market moves, is very important. Equally significant is knowing when currencies make their biggest moves. Although the Forex market can be traded, twenty-four hours a day, five and one-half days a week, some hours are better than others.

When starting to learn about currency trading, it is natural to want to learn the best strategies for success. Knowing how, and why a market moves, is very important. Equally significant is knowing when currencies make their biggest moves. Although the Forex market can be traded, twenty-four hours a day, five and one-half days a week, some hours are better than others.

One thing that many people do, is trade during times where two markets overlap. These times provide the highest volume, and volatility of trading; therefore, they are perfect for price action traders.

The Asian Session (Tokyo), is from 6 p.m. – 3 a.m. EST.

The European Session (London), is from 2 a.m. – 11 a.m. EST.

The North American Session (New York), is open from 7 a.m. – 3 p.m. EST.

The overlapping times are: 2 a.m. – 3 a.m. EST., and 7 a.m. – 11 a.m. EST. Some people do not start trading until the New York stock exchange opens at 9:30 a.m. EST., skipping the 2 ½ hours before that entirely.

A good habit I have developed is to check to see if there are any news announcements taking place during the time I will be trading. If there are, I look at what currency it will be affecting. My favourite website for this is, "Investing.com" **http://www.investing.com/economic-calendar/** This site grades the foreseeable impact by showing; one, two, or three bull skulls. Another great source of event times is, "Forex Factory." **http://www.forexfactory.com/** The website lists the announcements, and grades their expected impact as; low, (yellow) medium, (orange) and high (red).

These news releases, are frequently from governments around the world, releasing unemployment rates, housing sales, interest rate changes, just to name a few. It is best for new traders not to be in a trade during these times. With experience, you may start to capitalize on medium, and high-impact events.

Understanding the different characteristics of the times you trade.

If you trade different sessions, you should know a few basics. Let's start out with getting an understanding of what currency pairs will move the most, and at what times. North American sessions will see the biggest movement with pairs that have a USD or CAD in them. (typically) The Asian session should show more price action on the pairs that have, JPY or AUD, and the European Session will of course show more movement with pairs that have EUR and GBP.

The second thing you should note is, each session behaves differently. Some people love to trade the New York session, (North American) as it can show wild fluctuations, prices can move substantially. Others find it to be too volatile, and prefer the Asian session, which is typically calmer. I would recommend you watch different trading times, to learn their unique characteristics. You can then trade at the times that best suit your style.

Best and worst trade lengths.

One of the things that draw people to the world of Binary Options is watching examples of people growing their bank accounts in just minutes. As mentioned earlier, most brokers will allow you to trade expiry times from thirty seconds, to end of day, and many choices in-between. Most of the promotional videos you will see are one-minute trades. This is to get you excited, and demonstrate how fast it is possible to make money. What they don't tell you is, shorter trade lengths come with higher risks. A currency pair will fluctuate on its way up or down. What will a pair do in the next one minute? This can be very hard to foresee. It is much easier to predict where the pair will be in one hour. This does not mean you cannot follow a one-minute chart, I just would not typically take a trade this short. An exception to this rule is during news events I may take a two-minute option. My favorite way to trade, is to watch the five-minute chart and open a ten to fifteen-minute trade. This gives the pair some time to move in my predicted direction.

How To Avoid Being Scammed

All over the internet, there are people trying to scam you out of your money. In the Binary Options business, this is no different. The most common scams are:

All brokers will offer you a bonus for signing on. This bonus is usually 50% - 100% of your initial deposit. As inviting as this sounds, there is no "free" money. In the fine print, you will learn this money comes at a high price. You will be obligated to trade your investment, plus your bonus money between twenty to fifty times. (ex: If you invest $300, and your bonus is 50%, you now have $450. If that broker requires a thirty times trade volume requirement, you would need to trade $13,500.00 before you would be eligible to withdraw any money.) If you trade 5%, this would be $22.50 per trade. In order to meet your obligation, you would need to take 600 trades! The solution to this problem is simple, never accept the bonus. Talk with the broker before depositing any funds, to find out what steps you need to take to decline their bonuses.

This scam I can speak about to you from personal experience, having been on the losing end many times with my previous brokers. In an earlier section of this book, I discussed the differences between Forex and Binary fees, explaining how Forex brokers make money with spreads. Although many Binary brokers do not make money outright from spreads, they do in a sneakier way. After your trade has closed, you will see on some brokers, a message to the effect "calculating." What are they calculating you ask? The broker is looking at the "bid and ask price," for the time you entered your trade. Whichever price benefits them the most, is the one they will use for the final decision of whether you have won or lost. Not every trade moves by a large amount. The ones that move marginally, are where this scam applies. (ex: If the bid price was 1.08841 and the ask price was 1.08852 the price 1.08847 is what your broker would show. If you were to enter a CALL trade, and the price went in your expected direction, closing at 1.08849. Since this is below the ASK price, it would calculate as a loss. Even though your price did go up.)

Like the first example above, this is discussed somewhere in your "terms of service," of your Binary broker. The trouble is, few people read them, and fewer understand them. They are typically written in a way that is difficult for the layman to understand.

The last scam I want to talk about are the many robots/indicators/auto traders out there. They all make grand "get rich quick" statements. I have seen endless pop-ups, Youtube videos, and spam emails, promising a trading system that will make all who try it a millionaire. These are all scams! Some of them are free, some charge, but the one thing they all have in common, is they require you to sign-up with their broker. This is the sole purpose of these scams. There is nothing wrong with recommending a broker, and collecting affiliate commissions, but when the robots you are promoting, have little, to no value, you are being taken advantage of. If it sounds too good to be true, it probably is.

Signal Services

These services offer new traders a way to start trading without any knowledge of the market. Some companies email, or text you, while others will have you join a video conference so you can watch over-the-shoulder of a professional trader. Whichever delivery method used, you are given Currency pairs, Commodities, or Future Indices the professionals believe will be fluctuating in value soon. They will also tell you when, and for how long to take the trade.

Although this can be a good place to start, they are probably not where you will finish. The biggest problem being, you don't learn any skills. You are kept dependent on their services. Early in my trading experience, I joined a Skype group dedicated to Binary Options. It was here where I started to learn some strategies, and a bit about indicators. One of the members started a service where he not only gave signals, but also provided education. I became a student of his, and was later promoted to help him educate new traders. If you would like to learn more information about this group, please visit

http://trainingforbeginners.com/binaryoptions/

Conclusion

Having traded Binary Options for sometime now, I can honestly say the journey has been difficult, but an enjoyable one. If you choose to trade, please have realistic goals. Don't risk one child's college fund to make enough money to pay for another. Trading is difficult, and you will never "get rich quick" as all the scammers would have you believe. The sad truth is, most people will lose money, even with good strategies. If after reading this book you still wish to become involved in Binary Options, my advice to you would be to focus on Forex training, or find someone who specializes in Binary. All the successful traders I know, have an understanding of how traditional Forex works. Even if you focus your training on the one and five-minute charts, it is very beneficial to have a broader view and understanding of the markets. It would be like asking a doctor to diagnose a patient, but only give them selected information.

I will leave you with what I feel, are the seven steps every trader should follow.

Seven steps to make it in the world of Binary Options.

1. Never trade with money you can't afford to lose!!

2. Trade in the direction of the trend, "The trend is always your friend."

3. Know when to quit, some days you just can't win!

4. The more you think you know, the more at risk you are. Binary Options look simple, but are incredibly difficult. Always accept there is more to learn.

5. Short term trade movements are very fluid. Don't try to predict with pinpoint accuracy where an asset will go, accept the fact that the market moves in a very random way.

6. Be faithful to your trading rules, "consistency is king."

7. Only take trades that have a high probability of winning, wait for the good setups, and never trade just for the sake of making a trade.

Terminology

When first starting out, you may feel a bit lost, trading terminology is foreign to most people. Here is a list of the most common words, and abbreviations used in the trading community.

FX = Foreign exchange

Broker = The company you deal with for your Binary Options, or Forex investments.

Asset = Currency, Index, Commodity, or Stock that you are investing in.

ITM = In the money. (Is winning, or has won)

ITM% = This refers to the amount of money you will receive, if the trade wins. This is normally close to 75% with most brokers. (ex: You invest $100.00 and win, you would receive $175.00, your $100.00 back, plus the 75% for winning.)

OTM = Out of the money. (Is losing, or has lost)

OTM% = This refers to the amount you will get back, if the trade ends with a loss. Normally, you do not receive anything, some brokers do pay a small percentage.

Call = Up (ex: I bought a call option for EUR/USD)

Buy = Has the same meaning as Call, or Up.

PUT = Down (ex: I bought a put option for EUR/USD)

Sell = Has the basic same meaning as Put, or Down.

Bull = A bull, or bullish market, is one that is going up. There are more buyers than sellers.

Bear = A bear, or bearish market, is one that is going down. There are more sellers than buyers.

Trend = The direction an asset consistently moves.

Retracement = A temporary reversal in the direction of an asset. (ex: If EUR/USD has been dropping consistently on your five-minute chart, and you see it go up for a short time.)

Martingale = This refers to a trading strategy where after a loss, you would follow the trade with another, doubling your initial lost investment. (ex: $25.00 on EU that loses you would follow with a $50.00 trade. If this trade where to lose because at this point you would have lost $75.00 you would place a $150.00 trade.)

Support/Resistance = Also known as (S/R). This is a fundamental strategy most traders look for. "Support" is a zone that is below a current assets price, where the price frequently turns around. "Resistance" is a zone that is above a current assets price, where the price frequently turns around.

Trading Signals = A recommendation from a professional trader.

Forex Trading = Trading currency pairs in the foreign exchange market.

PIP (Price Interest Point) = A pip is 1/100th of 1%, a very small measure of change, in a currency pair in the Forex market. (ex: If EUR/USD went from 1.36290 to 1.36300 you could say it went up one PIP.) Anything smaller would be refereed to as a percentage of a PIP. Terminology

Resources

Charts.

Free Stock Charts — **http://www.freestockcharts.com/**

FxPro (MT4 charting software) — **http://www.fxpro.co.uk/**

News websites.

Forex Factory — **http://www.forexfactory.com/**

Investing.com — **http://www.investing.com/economic-calendar/**

Miscellaneous

All of the pictures in this book can be viewed at — **http://trainingforbeginners.com/binaryoptions/**

Binary Options Broker information, and the company I am involved with that educates can also be found at the above link.

Forex Reviews — **http://trainingforbeginners.com/forexreviews**

Greenshots — **http://getgreenshot.org/**

Printed in Great Britain
by Amazon